W9-ASD-494

Library of Congress Catalogue Card Number: 85-62090

Hardcover ISBN: 0-917631-01-3

Photographs © 1985. Copyright 1985 in U.S.A. by Chip Henderson.

This book, or portions thereof, may not be reproduced in any form without permission of the publishers, Capitol Broadcasting Company, Inc., and the producers of the book, Lightworks, Inc.

Photography may not be reproduced in any form without permission of Chip Henderson.

Printed in the state of North Carolina by Harperprints, Inc., Henderson, North Carolina.

Published in 1985 by Capitol Broadcasting Company, Inc., 2619 Western Boulevard, Raleigh, North Carolina 27605.

Produced and distributed through Lightworks, Inc., Raleigh, North Carolina. 919/851-0518 or 919/851-0512.

North Carolina
A Blessing Shared

Photography by Chip Henderson

Text and Captions by Glenn Morris

Design and Photographic Editing by Carolyn T. Strickland

Published by Capitol Broadcasting Company, Inc.

There is more than just distance between Manteo and Murphy. These two communities are the symbolic bookends of North Carolina. Between them is a shelf full of wonder 543 miles long.

Three volumes which read very differently rest on the shelf. North Carolina neatly parcels into the Coastal Plain, the Piedmont and the Mountains, distinctive geographic regions. Each has its own inherent beauty and cultural identity, which has been influenced by the lay of the land itself.

The Coastal Plain belongs to the plow and the bow of a boat. It is flat and fertile, easily fished and easily farmed. The crops of the Piedmont are the dreams and ambitions of entrepreneurs, who long ago harnessed the power of its rivers to generate commerce. The Mountains sequester rugged individualism and self reliance in their folds and vales. Mountain folk do what they must to remain in their cherished hills.

While there are many differences among these regions, several common threads bind them together, among them, the pace of life here and a genuine friendliness. But the most important link is this: North Carolinians are heirs to one of the most magnificent pieces of real estate in creation. The mountains, the piedmont and the coast belong to all of us and we will fiercely repel all threats to our heritage.

In our four hundred years of experience, we have learned how to live with the land, not against it. It is both our birthright and a firm but loving parent. It has shaped and molded our lives even as we shape and mold it to live here.

From Manteo east to Murphy west. From coastline to ridgeline, although we are many places and many people, we share a common blessing—North Carolina.

The Coast

The earliest shadow cast across North Carolina belongs to the Cape Hatteras Lighthouse, the easterly symbol of the state. Before it touches anything else in North Carolina, the rising sun strikes the top of this beacon and sends a shadow speeding across Hatteras woods, ironing across the rippling waters of Pamlico Sound.

Whether or not the shadow ever touches the mainland of the Coastal Plain is insignificant. But its racing direction is. It symbolizes the history of the state: North Carolina was discovered and settled east to west.

The touchstone of the English-speaking colonies is here — Roanoke Island, a wooded isle sheltered from the Atlantic's fury by the sandy necklace of the Outer Banks. West of Roanoke Island lies Croatan Sound. Its shallow waters join the two great waterways of settlement, Albemarle Sound to the north, Pamlico Sound to the south. Still further west from Roanoke Island begins the sloping near table-top flat land of the Coastal Plain mainland. This land still begs for the plow, and early on the winding rivers that inlay it beckoned for ships and sail.

North Carolina unfolded to explorers this way — from the gritty shoals of the Outer Banks, across shallow sounds to the comparatively high riverbank sites that became cities. Towns such as Hertford, Edenton, Washington, Bath, New Bern and Wilmington became the nucleus of an emerging state.

Setting history aside, the Coastal Plain province — the land from the Outer Banks west to the first rocky unnavigable falls of the rivers that thread it — has been unappreciated. Say "coast" in North Carolina, and everybody thinks beach, specifically the broad, sandy aprons of the barrier islands. Everything west of the beach is merely something through which to pass en route to the water. And there is plenty of water.

It sometimes seems as if nature created the Coastal Plain so water would have something to lap against and sky would have something to rest upon. There are wider horizons in the Coastal Plain than anywhere else in the state. Fully seven-eights of what you see is above you. The rest holds you up — either flat, farmable land or flat, fishable water.

To understand the Coastal Plain, you must understand flat and wide. Every other difference the eye discerns here is one of texture or color, or the height of something created by man.

The Coastal Plain is a beautiful mosaic: sun-bleached tidal marsh as broad as the eye can follow; level beach planing into the surf; mullet skipping on the water of the sound; boats of every size, shape and design; and magnificent flights of ducks and geese. Arrow-straight highways where rows of crops flicker past the window like pickets on a fence. A "howdy" at a country store. A region where tractors have the right-of-way and I-frame houses rule beneficently over farmland; where you can launch a hang glider from Jockey's Ridge or spend a red-eyed night fishing from a pier.

The Coastal Plain isn't easy. You have to work it to know it, east to west, surf to sound to silo. Ocracoke is part of it, as is Murphreesboro, Knott's Island and Kinston. But though it isn't easy, the land is receptive.

You can plow it, graze it, till it, timber it, fish it, trap it, swim it, and sail it. Bask in its warmth, boat it, run it, drive it and follow it through centuries by reading its history in church graveyards.

It is, above all, a land in community with water and plow, where the good earth and bountiful sea provide all the rewards needed to those who spill their sweat.

The barrier islands protect the harbors, and the inlets between them mark channels to port. The lighthouses of North Carolina are sacred sites for mariners, who view beacons such as the Bald Head Island Lighthouse as symbols of safe passage.

More protected and undeveloped coastline exists along North Carolina's barrier islands than along any other southeastern state. Your very own beach, sun, and solitude await at the top of a guardian dune.

The fish do not belong to the grizzled, long-armed and mighty. They belong to those who don't mind the pier walk and the wait. The wooden peninsulas known as piers bring man and sea together with a goal in

You have to climb Jockey's Ridge to believe it: two steps forward, one slide back. The light dances and the wind tugs at the eolian fragments rolling the sand over itself and the island. While its shape changes year after year, the pinnacle of Jockey's Ridge affords the most magical natural view of the Outer Banks, worth the plod to the top anytime.

The shrimper, Miss Sarah Helen, at rest. Perhaps before dawn she'll begin her steady ply back and forth across the teeming estuary of the sounds and shallower offshore waters. Like other shrimpers, her captain and crew fish until full or they can't fill at all. Feast or famine. But the shrimpers wouldn't trade the pungent odor of fishing for any perfume of nine to five.

This Southport fisherman pulls his livelihood from the sea — like his father, grandfather and perhaps even his great-grandfather before him. How many days out and the bounty he pockets for his risk and effort are whims of the ocean. Once safe and soundside, cleaning begins.

The skilled fingers that mend a net weave a livelihood as well. A sound net is all that stretches between a fisherman and his catch. Every rent in the fabric is a drain for wriggling life.

For a few fleeting weeks in summer, spartina, the marsh grass of the salt flats, is green. This is tidal water, ebbing and flowing. The pier that spans the life-giving marsh leads to a ride-giving channel, and what is born in the marsh returns in the boats that leave from it.

Neither the shape of the Outer Banks nor the surety of its channels is guaranteed. The only constant is the wind. The breathy blessing that propelled men of sail to their livelihood guides pleasure sailors today to a different reliance on the land of sky and water.

A waterman's boathouse at Bald Head Island is sound-side safe and elevated against the tides. It shares the peace and the elements of the sound. Now abandoned, it was once the home for a stout boat.

The Cape Hatteras Lighthouse, barber-poled and proud, is the tallest brick lighthouse in the world. It is perhaps the most cherished symbol of maritime history in this country, yet its days may be numbered because of erosion. What is the value of trying to save the Cape Hatteras Lighthouse from the forces of nature? Just ask the salts whose lives its beacon saved since 1870.

After marsh grass dies, it decomposes to become one of the most important links in the saltwater food chain that leads to man. For all this, it is silent, it is passive, and it is peaceful. Yet, it is life.

South of Cape Lookout the geography of the barrier islands takes a protective tuck to the west. Here, unlike most of the Coastal Plain, the sun rises and sets along the shoreline. It's tan time, big time, as long as you face the ocean, you are one with the sun.

Sometimes it is a short walk to the end of a pier but a long walk back. The distance is determined by the weight of the cooler — no fish, long walk.

The moods and sounds of the marsh at moonrise are eerily peaceful. It belies the importance of the marsh as the source of the coastal life cycle.

Swimming from sunrise to sunset is the rule of the coast, for there never again may come such a magical opportunity — until next summer.

Homeward bound. There is almost as much water as land in North Carolina's coastal counties. Pleasure craft abound in the protected waters of the state's many sounds. The sheltered mainland provides near countless safe harbors for fishermen and recreational sailers alike.

This is almost as far east as you can fish in North Carolina without getting caught in a four-wheel drive urban sprawl. Just south and east of this solitary angler is Cape Point, where the one fish might be that several hundred fishermen will pursue in customized off-road vehicles that are tackle shops on tires.

Two things will exist always on the barrier beaches — music and motion. The rolling cinema of the clouds plays to the metronome of the surf, over and over endlessly. Each dawn assures a new concert; today, adagio; tomorrow, vivace.

The challenge of the sea has always been this—to go and to return, whether for pleasure or for livelihood. You test your mettle against the flecks of foam to sail again.

In a tawny subdued world, enters man and the cats—Hobie cats—as close to being a dolphin as man will ever be. The rainbow sails hold promise of lightlike motion across salty waters.

Inlets teem with rich fishing, and the spit of sand curling south and west beneath the Herbert C. Bonner Bridge is a prime access point for Oregon Inlet anglers. Inlets and sand spits come and go; but so do fish, jeeps and fishermen and dusk — it is a combination as old and true as the state.

This is fishing's moment. It comes early in the day; it comes late; it may never come at all. But when it does, it is the reward for countless hours of waiting, early rising and trekking through soft sand. The split second, set your jaw to set a hook, the reaction to action. Jerk, reel hard and pray for bragging rights.

The play, *The Lost Colony*, presented annually since 1937, commemorates an event which unfolded 400 years ago on Roanoke Island. It dramatizes the first attempt to establish an English-speaking colony in the New World.

Among the several truths of the coast is this: every day, every golden-toned day provides a chance for replenishment and restitution for man, creature and the very beach itself. Clear dawns are a communion of earth and heaven.

Across Ocracoke Inlet lies Portsmouth Island and the abandoned village of Portsmouth. Once an important port of entry, Portsmouth today is only a prim, three-building community in Cape Lookout National Seashore. It is visited monthly by shellers, tourists and fishermen.

An unflappable island feline perches atop the most famous picket fence on Ocracoke Island — it borders the walk to the oldest continuously operating lighthouse in the state. Oh, for the life of an Ocracoke cat.

The First Presbyterian Church in Wilmington is one of the denomination's oldest congregations in the state. Its burnished handrails have been polished by the touch of reverent assemblages of several generations. There is a patina of faith on the balustrade alone.

The transition beach, from winter to summer, leaves the remnants of a protective offshore bar that thwarts winter wave energy. That bar creates tidal pools, and the tidal pools trap small fish. It is a sanderling's paradise.

Those who visit Ocracoke inevitably wait for the ferry, but they are not the only ones. The question is not who is waiting for the ferry but, while waiting, who is watching whom. Easy answer — the gulls are the watchers. They soar free waiting for no man.

Fort Fisher was the site of a major Union assault during the Civil War. Today, its bastions against the sea are the sites of a more simple struggle – that between man and fish.

The Piedmont

The Piedmont, the heart of North Carolina, is a region that rolls steadily westward and upward from the Fall Line to the first abrupt walls of the Blue Ridge Mountains. This is white-collar country, where many North Carolinians live and work in a great belt of population centers that arches from Raleigh in the east, northwest through Durham, Greensboro and Winston-Salem, and south and west from there to Charlotte. Linked by ribbons of interstate highways and stitched with rail lines, these cities barter with computer chips, furniture and textiles as readily as their eastern and western neighbors swap bushels of produce and hundredweights of tobacco.

If you live in a Piedmont city, you can spend all day in a boat or on horseback and still get home in time to shower and attend a symphony. Stated another way, you can dove hunt within beeper range.

This proximity of the best of urban and rural living is important to remember. Such technology as a beeper hanging on a belt at an afternoon shoot is a newcomer to the region but an important indicator of recent changes.

As little as thirty years earlier, the Piedmont's cities were compact, self-contained islands of commerce in an agricultural sea. City limits contained gravelled streets and milkmen clanked through the early dew of dawn on daily routes. Just a memory's blink ago, physicians took payment in bushel baskets and children crowded downtown theaters to cheer through serialized westerns.

There were city dwellers then of course, but no urban culture per se. A strong rural rhythm set the pace of life. While the rest of the nation commuted, Piedmont professionals merely went to work.

It was a secret too good to keep. Piedmont cities, the twentieth century descendants of sleepy-little towns, awakened to find that they were much preferred locations. Business and cultural centers sprouted on ridgelines; homes and suburbs spilled outward into the country from central business districts lining streets that dip and roll. National and international corporations discovered what you already knew — the Piedmont is one of the top-rated locations in the country if the yard-stick measures quality of life. People are finding their place in the sun in the Piedmont — they need it for a garden. But they are finding ample shade as well and four distinct seasons that grace the region with enough snow in winter and sun in summer to satisfy almost anyone.

Growing up in the Piedmont can spoil you. You can reach either the mountains or the coast with relative ease. The Piedmont is a consummate compromise between these extremes and its inhabitants can look both east and west with pride. They can love both ends of the state with the fervency of a lifelong resident.

There are some of the best features of urban living here — education, industry, medical resources and cultural events. And always, just down the road, or over the next hill, or around the next bend, is the land from which modern-day North Carolina sprung as though launched by a tightly wound spring.

In the Piedmont, Monday through Friday belongs to neckties and stoplights, but Saturday and Sunday belong to blue jeans and farm-to-market roads. It is indeed a nice place to live, all the more so because you realize what lies just beyond the city-limit signs.

"Betchacantbeatme." The furrows of this Bladen County soybean field have become the track for a clog-laden race, settling the speed of farmers-to-be. Its rows are as true as surveyor's lines— beans don't do well in curves.

There is one unquestionable fact about the small farm communities of the Piedmont (and elsewhere in the state): the proper forum for settling the issues of the day is a screen porch. It has a door that is open to the world, but the opinions voiced in its shadows will never penetrate the mesh.

The people of Spring Hope wanted a festival, and Elmo Tant gave them a reason — his "punkins." They are inevitably orange, inevitably large and indisputably fall.

In fall, sometimes everybody is so busy trying to get to the mountains that they forget to look beneath their feet. There, the rainbows of the woods become the carpet of home.

54

A treasured, favorite chair. Favored not so much for its construction but because it serves well. It performs as chairs do well, not letting its owner down, in a manner of speaking. Someone, perhaps long ago and yet not so far away, made this chair memorable. Not so much for the sitting but for the love and the wisdom dispensed from the worn seat.

These work-marked hands hold the promise of an entire town — the seeds that when carefully sown, cultivated, loved and orated over will become the guests of honor at the Spring Hope Pumpkin Festival.

Dark green on light, or light green on dark? No matter — either way
they surround watermelon pink. Or do they? An old North Carolina
adage asserts that "a watermelon is white on the inside until you cut it."
To the best of our collective folk wisdom, this remains true to this day.

There simply is no urgency in the business of watermelons. Everything about them is lazy: the growing, the waiting, the harvesting and the selling. So, why not relax, as this vendor at the Raleigh Farmer's Market does, and let the watermelons do best what only they can do—sell themselves.

This is the day of reckoning. A tobacco farmer works 13 months of the year for his payoff. The thirteenth month is called "Tobaccorary" and falls in the calendar whenever there is more to do than time allows. As this farmer shows, nothing is better than a smoke to relieve the tension of an auction.

A plow cuts straight, even and deep when there are no hills to fight. Indeed, it cuts right up to the back, front and sides of many a farmhouse. Every square foot of arable soil is precious to farm families for, except in hard times, the more in seed, usually the more in the bank and the hand.

At the Pinehurst/Southern Pines equestrian center, a stablehand — Eastern Cowboy — boasts the same red-cheeked countenance and Stetson of his western counterparts.

During the cool of an early morning outing, this horse and rider functioned as one. The horse exercised his supple body; the rider honed his mastery of the animal's rhythm and strength. Now heading into the shaded comfort of a stall, the rider will begin to repay his mount for their moments of motion.

This photograph was taken in the early morning, but it already was too late in the day to catch the residents on their way to work. North Carolina may have more small farms than any other state, and the farm home is the heart of the agrarian economy.

The orb weavers spin their gossamer traps at night and each day brings a newly threaded geometry. Sometimes these spiderly nets trap something other than prey. This one has snared the dew. Surely man has never fashioned jewelry as finely crafted as this diadem of morning.

The major lakes of the Piedmont region are impoundments, created to provide flood control, water supply or a source of power. These reservoirs produce fish and scenery as well. Before the completion of Falls Lake north of Raleigh, there was no suitable mirror for this autumn woodland.

Cycads grow successfully in one place in North Carolina—the R. J. Reynolds Free-Flight Aviary in Asheboro. The award-winning geodesic dome brings people into the world of 100 bird and 80 plant species. It is like walking through an immense terrarium, where any color other than green belongs to a creature that flies and sings.

An international world of wildlife has magically appeared in the rock-strewn land south of Asheboro. The North Carolina Zoological Society is creating one of the foremost zoological parks in the world on a 1500-acre site just south of the geographic center of the state. So naturalistic are its habitats that reptilians such as these are oblivious to their observers. Who is watching whom? The contented animals at the zoo couldn't care less.

On the Capitol Square in Raleigh are two living fixtures: the pigeon, ever a capitalistic bird, and the pigeon man. The pigeon man sells peanuts to passersby, who pass them to the pigeons which have been continuously in session since the building was completed as the legislators' roost in 1840.

The Piedmont can rely on one school-closing, traffic-busting snowfall each winter. Everything comes to a standstill and there is the opportunity to take the time to read the crystalline calligraphy of snow on tree limbs.

There is nothing like the midway of the North Carolina State Fair: a neon roller coaster, lights, action and reverie. After the judging, after the best apple pie, blue-ribbon chowchow and prize steer have received their honors, then, and only then, come the cotton candy, teddy bears and spins through the heavens on the fabulous rides.

A contestant gives one last bath to a cherished sheep before the judging at the State Fair in Raleigh. Held every year in the middle of October, the month traditionally given to harvest, the fair celebrates and honors the agricultural heritage of the state. The best of the best— sheep, Duroc boars, Holsteins, Herefords, Rhode Island Reds, pumpkins, yams, and apples—compete for top honors.

Every October, Statesville hosts one of the largest hot-air balloon rallies in the nation. It is perhaps the most spectacular outdoor event in the state. Slowly, these great pouches of color awake at dawn to hover silently over a shimmering autumn countryside. It may be the only time in the year when there is more color in the sky than there is on the trees.

This helmeted gentleman has good reason for wearing such a calm expression: he has both the hillsides of the Piedmont and the updrafts of its heavens at his command. From a hot air balloon, a patchwork of woods and fields unfolds. And, if the view from above doesn't saturate the mind, then consider a view of the viewer, who is one with the clouds.

North Carolina has adopted some aristocratic ways and made them events with a local flavor, none more so than the equestrian competitions of Southern Pines and Pinehurst. At these competitions, initiated by wealthy individuals of the Northeastern states who found fine riding in the sandhills here, the decor, dress and dressage reign supreme—not to mention the fox and hound, of course.

Where there are foxes and open country, there are men and horses in pursuit. The soft sands of Southern Pines are easy on the hooves of mounts. There's cover for the clever quarry, the fox. So the hunt, with all its trapping, has found a stable environment just two hours south of Raleigh.

This volunteer in Winkler's Bakery, in the heart of the restored Moravian settlement of Salem, North Carolina, is dressed in simple, traditional Moravian garb. She serves one and all with the same hospitality once exuded by the original inhabitants of Salem. The work, fare, dress and life-style of the Moravians was humble and simple. They worked only for a peace with God.

The Moravians were a pacifistic people whose communal way of life centered around their Protestant belief. Their many talents included ceramics, music, brewing and cooking. Their baking may still be sampled today at Winkler's.

Fourth of July at the North Carolina State Fairgrounds is a come-as-you-are; eat-what-you-can; play-as-you-will hullabaloo. Here, a tumble of hands and feet heads toward an ice-cold watermelon finish.

Everybody loves a parade and a band, but nobody more than Cary. Cary, just west of Raleigh, has more collective brass than any other city in the state during its Band Days. Students from all over the nation march to the beat of a different drummer hoping to stride away, rhythmically, with the top prize.

In the heart of booming Raleigh, citizens are discovering the soul of the city's past. Historic Oakwood is a neighborhood renaissance story looking to its past to build a future. More than old houses have been restored; residents also have dusted off earlier values, such as community pride. Likely, the apple pie is still in the oven.

Long before there were coiffures for men, there were barbers. Do not be misled into thinking that all a barber does is cut hair. In a small town such as Louisburg, the barbershop serves as the equivalent of an Associated Press wire service. All that is current is passed through the barber, quietly repeated over the artful snip of a master's scissors.

Now firmly a part of the governmental mall in Raleigh, the Seaboard Coastline Building came within a hairbreadth of the wrecking ball. The entire building was moved to its permanent site to be used for office space. A Greek revival architectural masterpiece, the building is noted for its fine wrought-iron railings and classic facade.

Fishing a lake is essentially a solitary affair, a time that is contemplative by nature. Among other thoughts might be the fact that fifteen years ago nobody would have dreamed of catching a fish in the top of a tree.

The Mountains

The mountains of western North Carolina come closer to the heavens than any other region in the East. On a summer's day, this part of North Carolina literally has its head in the clouds. Haze enfolds the mountain tops, and you can't see a thing. It is only when the dawning or setting sun gleams through the mist that the separate ridgelines and their many layers of rock become distinct to the eye.

In winter, cold weather plants the clouds low in the valleys. Above them, the sky is blue and clear and crisp as hoarfrost. Ridgeline after ridgeline marches outward from your vantage point. The price for this vision is a cold that will sting and water your eyes, and through chill-tears, the land corrugates like a washboard. You can scrub your soul clean with the sight of it.

Driving through the mountains is like unwrapping a package. Each turn in the road reveals something new. But unlike a present, there is no prize; instead, the unwrapping itself is the gift. One good bend promises another, and for every hillside dappled with Holsteins another awaits in rhododendron pink. You can't lose regardless of the turn you take, but the road less traveled is the one that holds the treasures.

An old adage is especially true in the hill and vale country: if you ain't going somewhere, you can't get lost. If your eyes are open, you'll find something everywhere you look.

You'll have plenty of time for looking in the mountains because a decidedly deliberate attitude governs travel there. Admittedly, the hills alone dictate slower speeds, but there is something greater which actually sets your pace—an inherent truth of the mountains. Each day brings something new from these ancient weathered piles of rock. You can't see all of it in a lifetime, but you can't see any of it if you hurry.

The North Carolina tall country breeds strong people and tall tales. You have to be tough and independent to take the weather, let alone the steep ups and downs. You live either on top of a mountain, at the foot of a mountain or hung on the side like a squirrel on an oak.

Just learning to handle the literal ups and downs of daily living has made mountainfolk clannish. Life here can be hard enough without having to deal with the outside world. Thus, mountaineers—true mountaineers, not transplants—may seem standoffish, even suspicious. This manner is a legacy from earlier times, because they've seldom been approached by someone who didn't want something, usually the family's land. And their land is about all they've ever had, besides a good woodburning stove, an apple tree and a garden. What else do you need? Self-sufficiency is the heart of the proud mountaineer. Taking care of his own is the mark of his success. Failure to do so is the worst of local sins.

These rugged mountainfolk have learned some things that all of us should know: that flowers of bloodroot hold the promise of spring and that a late frost and a summer drought can put your back up against the woodpile during winter. That even during the snowiest, bitterest winter seasons, the mountains will sequester you in their vale like a benevolent parent. That you have to be resilient here to thrive. And that something as old and weathered as these hills will, at the very least, cradle your faith.

The mountains give, and the mountains take. To protect and keep their birthright, the mountaineers have learned to give back.

So must all of us.

The Blue Ridge Mountains. It is no more possible to count the ridgelines than it is to count the waves at sea. Both are endless or, at the
very least, indiscernable to the human eye. Yet, viewing each brings
a remarkable feeling of peace and comfort. Some things, such as
these weathered slumped hills, will endure far beyond our follies.

His hand on the gate leading to his property, this Valle Crucis farmer symbolizes much of what is true about the mountains. This is his land, his farm — from broad expanse of field to every minute detail of his house. A man's worth is measured not so much by the amount of his land but by the condition of it. A good pasture has little broom sage.

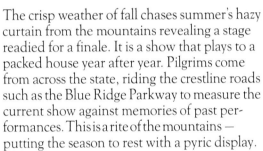

The crisp weather of fall chases summer's hazy curtain from the mountains revealing a stage readied for a finale. It is a show that plays to a packed house year after year. Pilgrims come from across the state, riding the crestline roads such as the Blue Ridge Parkway to measure the current show against memories of past performances. This is a rite of the mountains — putting the season to rest with a pyric display.

What is snow on the outside of Winebarger's Mill in Meat Camp, North Carolina, might as well be flour on the inside. Same texture, different temperature and substance, it dusts both exterior and interior, as the ghosted miller reveals. The miller lives in dust — the pure, sweet dust of sustenance. Round and round goes the water wheel and, inevitably, the measure of man's production — his worth for a season comes out on the scales. The miller takes his cut; the balance goes to market.

On this pyrotechnic night, campers on the bald highlands of the North Carolina-Tennessee border dance with the fire in the air. They cannot run, nor hide, nor make it stop. Instead, they bask in the sweet ozone and pray for a reprieve from a lull in common sense.

Occasionally, but not as a rule, the rivers have flattened the ancient hill-sides of these mountains into something that a Piedmont farmer would consider plowable. Such bottomland always tails a stream, and it is rare and valuable. It becomes prime, intense farmland — growing hay for silage, corn for silage, cabbage for market or tobacco for the curing barn. In this country, flat land means rich land.

A gourd is a very useful product in the mountains. A practical vegetable gone chic. You can dip water with a gourd, or plant flowers in it, or invite birds to live there. Gourds have many uses. These are "designer gourds," mountain-style, grown because they've always been grown; besides, they're just pretty to look at.

Truck farming takes a 180-degree twist in the mountains, the truck doesn't move, you drive to it. Roadside stands are a part of the life and lore of the serpentine roads. Here is the best cider, sourwood honey or quilts — every humble, nonabrasive sort of retail. Here, also, is a person's life. You rarely are hard-pressed to buy; it is assumed that you know what you want. If you don't it's your own tomfoolery, and there is little time to be wasted on you.

This High Hampton morning dawn comes with a mist rising from the
lake in the valley floor. Beyond the shrouded surface, Whitesides
Mountain waits for the amber glow of sunrise to blaze its sheer 1500
foot wall. It is one of the finest wake-up calls in the state.

Nowhere else are the mountain folk more clannish than at the Scottish Games at Grandfather Mountain; and nowhere else is a fling really a fling. This lass is paying the piper as only dancers do. She must turn on a dime with a ballerina's grace and the posture of a statue; there must be a spring in her step that is cat-quick and light as a feather. She dances for her clan, an expanded family with a heritage as tightly knit as its tell-tale tartan.

A backpacker's water fountain, Great Smoky Mountains National Park. There is no finer, colder drink than the spring-generated hillside waters. The pressure is there, and the pipe brings the flow to thirsty hikers.

If one plant rules the mountains, it is the rhododendron. Although there are several species of this genus in the state, it is only on the high balds, such as Roan Mountain, that the plant reigns with flamboyant dignity. It is first lush, then rich, then pink, then extraordinarily at peace in the sleet, cold and mist.

The cows long gone, the pasture ridgeline
bids the day farewell.

The deep greens and rushing sounds of a high-altitude forest blend
naturally to create a chapel-like feeling. Everything appears ordered and
undisturbed, and one feels a graciousness at being allowed to intrude.

Evidence points to the fact that the hard work of water has already been accomplished at Linville Falls. Not satisfied that it has gorged one of the great incisions in rock in America, the Linville River continues its steady cut a crystal at a time, and the gorge ever deepens.

It is all downhill from the mountains — an obvious statement where water is concerned, but perhaps the most important remark governing the shape of the mountains. The gentle fall shown here — a mud-stirring, soul-cleaning wash — carries the mountains to the sea particle by particle. Water is patient and where it meets a hard spot, it falls. In time, it will wear the obstruction that makes it tumble to a billiard-ball smooth surface.

All of us dream of summer retreats, but few of us have accomplished the dream to the extent that George Vanderbilt did with his fabulous Asheville estate, Biltmore. Richard Morris Hunt crafted the building, Frederick Law Olmstead crafted the grounds, and Vanderbilt's wealth gilded the already beautiful lily. There is no finer mansion in America.

Riding a rocket — the Nantahala River. Some of the best white-water rafting in the country is in North Carolina. Besides the Nantahala, there is the Nolichucky River and the Little Tennessee. If you want to leave the mountains in a hurry, take the rivers, not the highways.

Just beyond the major falls is one of the first wilderness areas in the Eastern United States— Linville Gorge. Near the resort town of Boone, it is a gash in the mountains that belongs to the far West. It is a true canyon with but a few ways down and out and a river to gobble your mistakes. Wiseman's View Overlook, on the western rim south of the falls, offers one of the most breathtaking views in the state.

The next generation. Face, place and time do not matter here. What is important is the continuity implied but never spoken. Perhaps this lad is a next-generation miller, farmer, cooper or wood-carver. More than likely, the mountains will become his home, and he will set up shop on the land of his ancestors.

What finer view from the window of a church than a mountain road. No stained glass is needed here. The road is a reminder of the humble path life should follow.

This is the mile-high swinging bridge at Grandfather Mountain. This is also, one of Grandfather Mountain's famous October fogs — famous for fog, not limited to October. The bridge is a catwalk. It links man of today with more than 600 million years of geologic history, winnowing his pride with the majesty of unfathomable time.

There may be more concentrated and collected energy in a sack race than any other carnival moment. More fun and giggles too.